ק"ק כנסת ישראל

UNITED SYNAGOGUE.

———

THE HISTORY OF

THE

BOROUGH SYNAGOGUE

COMPILED BY

THE REV. M. ROSENBAUM

TO COMMEMORATE THE FIFTIETH
ANNIVERSARY OF THE CONSECRATION
OF THE BOROUGH NEW SYNAGOGUE
IN HEYGATE STREET, WALWORTH, S.E.
NISAN 2, 5677—MARCH 25, 1917

Officers, 5677-1917

Wardens:

J. BERNBERG, ESQ.

H. BERNHARDT COHEN, ESQ.

Financial Representative:

A. A. LOGETTE, ESQ.

Representatives at the Council:

P. BRYMAN, ESQ.   E. S. ISRAEL, ESQ.

Board of Management:

D. BARNARD, ESQ.	E. S. ISRAEL, ESQ.
P. BRYMAN, ESQ.	M. LEVENE, ESQ.
A. EMDON, ESQ.	H. RAZANSKY, ESQ.
M. GOLDING, ESQ.	L. REDWOOD, ESQ.
A. HARRISON, ESQ.	E. M. TRAVIS, ESQ.

And the Wardens and Financial Representative *ex officio*.

Representative at the Board of Deputies:

H. BERNHARDT COHEN, ESQ.

Minister:

REV. M. ROSENBAUM.

Reader:

REV. E. FRANK.

Choirmaster:

MR. HARRY J. ROSENBAUM.

Beadle and Collector:

MR. BERNARD COHEN.

PREFACE.

GREAT difficulty has been experienced in writing an account of the early history of the Synagogues in the Borough. The only old record preserved is an account book covering the period 1823 to 1867, but the bearing of the entries upon the congregational history is not always clear. Much contained in the following pages could not have been written but for the kind assistance of Mr. Nathan Levi, a grandson of Mr. Nathan Henry, one of the first Jewish settlers in South London. The file of the *Jewish Chronicle* was readily placed at my disposal by the Editor, and much information has been obtained by direct communication with gentlemen who have been prominently associated with the Synagogue, Messrs. E. A. Cohen, J. A. Cohen, Philip Ornstien, and B. Cohen, and Mrs. A. Levy, to all of whom my cordial thanks are hereby tendered, whilst the personal recollections of the late Mr. Moss Benjamin and the late Mr. Benjamin Lyons, as recounted by them when I caught them in a reminiscent mood, have been most helpful.

M. ROSENBAUM.

Adar, 5677.
February, 1917.

THE HISTORY OF
THE BOROUGH SYNAGOGUE

THE precise period when Jews first settled in South London it is
now impossible to determine. Several names of Jewish
residents are to be found in the lists of subscribers printed in editions
of the Festival Prayers (Machsorim), published towards the end of the
eighteenth and the beginning of the nineteenth centuries. These
lived in the "Borough," a term designating a larger area than at
present, comprising, as it did, the whole of the main road from London
Bridge as far as the beginning of the Kennington Park Road, with all
the thoroughfares adjoining it. Others resided in Blackfriars and
Lambeth, and all were said to live "over the water," a delightfully
vague name for the district on the South side of the River.

Tradition has it that at one time the local Jewish residents repaired
to the King's Bench Prison, in the Borough, for divine service, the
unfortunate debtors incarcerated there helping to form the quorum
necessary for public worship (Minyan), which the Jews of the Borough
could not themselves muster. On these occasions a Mr. Lewis
(popularly known as "Captain" Lewis, grandfather of the late Sir
George Lewis, the celebrated solicitor) used to preside at the Reading
of the Law. About the year 1799 a Mr. Nathan Henry, the son of
Henry Abrahams, a connection of the well-known family of Hebrew
printers and booksellers, permitted a room in his house to be used as
a Synagogue. He resided at 2 Market Street (now Dantzic Street)—
a street leading out from Newington Causeway and running parallel
with London Road—at its junction with London Street. Nathan
Henry was born in 1764 or 1765, and as a lad of fifteen had heard
Lord George Gordon, who afterwards became a proselyte to Judaism,
addressing meetings in St. George's Fields, which were facing his

parents' house. Some years later he roofed in the whole of the yard at the rear of his house and shop, fitted the enclosure as a Synagogue, defraying all the expenses thus incurred. He himself officiated at the services, being assisted only on the High Festivals. Amongst those who, at different periods, read the Festival Prayers was Nathaniel Jessel, uncle of the famous Master of the Rolls. Entrance to the Synagogue was gained by the shop, which was an old-iron store, and thence through the " shop parlour," and the ladies had to ascend the stairs leading from this room to a bedroom above, through which they passed into the tiny gallery, which contained but two rows of seats. It was a modest building, which served its purpose for many years. In 1845 it was substantially repaired, and then provided accommodation for 100 persons, being described as "extremely small." The Treasurer, John Henry Lyons, held himself responsible for the cost of the repairs—some £40—towards which the sum of £23 was collected at the re-consecration.

There seems to be no doubt but that the worshippers at this small Synagogue contributed towards the expenses entailed by its upkeep. Nathan Henry, however, always styled himself the " proprietor " of the Synagogue, claiming the right of appointing its Wardens, since he had erected it at his own cost. Several regular worshippers who favoured a more democratic rule seceded from this congregation, and in 1823 they rented a building at the beginning of St. George's Road, near the " Elephant and Castle." This portion of the road was then known as Prospect Place, and the Synagogue was situated at the end of a short court between the buildings numbered 91 and 92 Prospect Place. It is probable that they had a meeting-place in the same locality a few years earlier than 1823. The leader of these secessionists was Mr. Aaron Cohen, father of Mr. Edward A. Cohen and Mr. John A. Cohen, who are still happily with us, having remained members of the Borough Synagogue although long resident in another part of the Metropolis. Mr. Aaron Cohen became Treasurer of the new congregation, and held this office for more than fifty years, until immediately after the erection of the present Borough Synagogue. Thus, the association of the father and sons with the Borough Congregation covers a period of just one century.

The congregation came into possession of the building, which, it seems, was originally intended for use as stables, towards the end of 1823, and services were held almost immediately. A sum of about

£40 was expended in adapting it for the purposes of a Synagogue, and the consecration took place in September, before the High Festivals, one guinea being paid to the Chazan who officiated and a similar sum to the "Singer," a Mr. Marks. A lease of the building was taken in 1826, and the account book of that year describes the congregation as באָרא מנין דחדשה (the "Borough New Minyan.") The Presidents were then Mr. W. Simmonds and Mr. L. Levy.

In 1831, when the Synagogue was rebuilt, in all likelihood only as regards its interior, at a cost of £230, towards which sum £163 was received from subscriptions, the congregation was indebted to the Treasurer to the amount of £78, of which £13 was on account of ordinary Synagogue expenditure. This rebuilding was followed by a re-consecration, and a similar ceremony took place in 1841, when some alterations were effected. Among the prominent seatholders at this early period was Mr. Baruch Cohen, grandfather of Mr. Neville D. Cohen. In 1827, his wife presented a handsome curtain for the Ark, and this was renovated sixty years later by their son, Mr. David Cohen. All the members of Mr. Cohen's family, and his kinsmen, the Levys, were associated with the Synagogue at that time. The descendants of both families have held responsible positions in the congregations of Liverpool and Sydney (New South Wales), as well as distinguished public offices in these cities, and it is a curious coincidence that the two present Ministers of the latter congregation were taken directly from the Borough Synagogue, the selection being in the hands of members of these two families.

In 1830, Nathan Ornstien had become an official of the congregation, although he had been connected with it in some minor capacity since 1823. He was a native of Nymegen, in Holland, a good Hebrew scholar, possessing the Hatorath Horoah (Rabbinical Diploma), and was affectionately known as "Rabbi Noson." His name disappears from the books in 1850, and his son, Phineas, succeeded him in an honorary capacity, becoming the paid Secretary in 1862, in which office his son, Philip Ornstien, the present Secretary of the United Synagogue, served for a short time in 1885, pending the appointment of a permanent Secretary. The general factotum of the congregation —Reader, Secretary, and Collector—was Joseph J. Phillips, quite a personage in his way, who, from the establishment of the congregation until his death in 1862, combined with his Synagogual duties the secretaryship of one or two local Jewish organisations, in addition to his avocation of a repairing jeweller. The congregation was usually in debt to the Treasurer, and it was only in 1846 that for the first time it had a small balance on the right side. The Presidents were then Mr. B. L. Phillips and Mr. J. Joseph, while Messrs. M. Harris, P. Cohen, and J. A. Ellis were members of the Committee. In 1847, some alterations, probably in the way of seatings, were made to the building. In 1848, the actual income was £110, the expenditure being less than £100. In 1853, there was a sudden rise in the income, this being £189, although it fell again next year, rising again in 1856, and then steadily increasing. This large increase in 1853 was due to a payment of £50 in July of that year. Nathan Henry had died on Eyar 4, 5613 (May 12, 1853), at the age of 88, and the little Synagogue in his garden ceased to be used within a couple of months of his death. For some years previously much difficulty had been experienced in collecting a congregation on Sabbaths, besides his own family only two or three residents attending regularly. His death merely hastened the inevitable closing of his Synagogue, most of its members joining the Prospect Place Synagogue, and the greater part of the £50 was, it may be assumed, a balance handed over by the Market Street congregation.

The relations between the two congregations were always of a cordial character. There must have been some transactions between Nathan Henry and the Prospect Place Synagogue at its very inception, for the first two entries in the account book of the latter are records of small sums paid to him in November and December, 1823. What these were for it is now impossible to ascertain. Nathan Henry himself was on friendly terms with the leaders of the other Synagogue, but it is said that he never set foot within their place of worship. Although the newer congregation was certainly the larger, the Market Street Synagogue alone received the official recognition of the Ecclesiastical Authorities. Thus, when Dr. Nathan M. Adler, some few months after entering upon his duties as Chief Rabbi, visited the Borough, on November 30, 1845, it was the Market Street Synagogue that he honoured. In an address on that occasion, the Chief Rabbi said :—

> "This minor temple has been erected nearly half a century.
> . . . Those who frequent this, are all of them, more or less,
> subscribing members to either the one or the other Synagogues in
> London and its vicinities. . . . The founder of this Synagogue

". . . did devote a portion of his habitation to the service of God so that his co-religionists might not be without a House of Prayer."

Nathan Henry was then eighty years of age, and was regarded as the head of the Jews in the Borough, and it was, perhaps, due to the respect in which he was held, as well as to the influence of his nephew, the Rev. H. A. Henry, of the Western Synagogue, St. Alban's Place, Haymarket, that his Synagogue was considered to be the official Synagogue in the South of London. At the time of this visit the Wardens were Mr. D. Daniels and Mr. L. Goldsmid, and the Treasurer Mr. J. H. Lyons. So far as is known, the Chief Rabbi never visited the Prospect Place Synagogue during the whole forty-four years of its existence.

The Jews of the Borough had other institutions besides their Synagogues. In 1812 there was established the " Tent of Righteousness " Friendly Society, which assured to its members payment of a weekly sum during sickness, besides Shiva and death benefits. Seatholders of both Synagogues were amongst its members and officers. The Society existed down to 1913, when it amalgamated with the South London Lodge of the Order Achei B'rith, one of the larger Jewish friendly organisations which have come into being during recent times. Some particulars regarding its origin and history will be found in the *Jewish Chronicle* of January 10, 1913, in connection with the celebration of its centenary.

The present Borough Synagogue preserves a ragged and faded slip of paper, containing a written announcement in Yiddish and English of the proposed establishment of a charitable society. The English version, in its quaint orthography, reads as follows :—

" Several Members of this Congregation are now erecting a Society for the casual Relief of Distresed Isralites who reside in Southwark, the Comitte trust it will meett with the support of Benevolent.

" This Society will commence Receiving subscriptions on the first Day of the ensuing סליחות

" August 15, 1825.

" J. PHILLIPS, *Secretary.*"

This was, in all probability, the society that was afterwards known as the " Surrey Jewish Philanthropic Institution," and, still later, as the " Surrey Philanthropic Society for Relieving Persons of the Jewish Persuasion." In the middle of last century it used to meet in St. George's Road, at the house of Mrs. Levy, mother of David Lewis, the well-known philanthropist of Liverpool. Subscribers were entitled to participate in a drawing twice annually for cash or grocery, which the winners were expected to distribute among the deserving poor. The Society was still in existence in 1869, when it was permitted to hold its meetings in the Committee room of the present Synagogue.

From 1853 the Prospect Place Synagogue remained the sole house of prayer for the Jews resident on the South side of the River. From this date it flourished, becoming the proud possessor in 1855 of £75 worth of Three per cent. Annuities Reduced Stock, to which it added almost every year until in 1865 its holding amounted to £500. At the beginning of 1862 Mr. Phineas Ornstien became Secretary and Collector, and old Joe Phillips retired on an annuity of £21 per annum after almost forty years' service. He lived to enjoy his well-earned rest less than two years, dying on January 19, 1864, at the age of 71. In the announcement of his death in the *Jewish Chronicle*, he is described as the Rev. Mr. Joseph J. Phillips. He was never married, and by his will he bequeathed £50 to the Borough Synagogue, £10 to the New Synagogue, and similar amounts to the Institution for the Blind, the Initiation Society, and the Orphan Asylum. He had previously presented a curtain for the Ark and various prayer books for the use of the Reader of the Synagogue. In 1862, also, appears in the books for the first time the name of the Rev. Solomon Levy as Reader. One of his sons is the Rev. Dr. J. Leonard Levy, Rabbi of the Rodeph Shalom Congregation at Pittsburgh. The accounts for 1865 record the receipt of a legacy of £50 from Mr. Z. A. Jessel, grandfather of the late Mr. Albert H. Jessel, for twenty-five years President of the Borough Jewish Schools.

In September, 1866, the lease of the Synagogue expired, and the sum of £70 was paid to Messrs. Drake and Son on account of dilapidations. For some years back much consideration had been given to the question of erecting a new Synagogue, and a Building Committee had been appointed in 1865, at the head of which was Mr. Barnett Meyers, a gentleman who did not reside in South London, but was a well-known and highly esteemed co-religionist possessing great influence with the wealthier members of the community. Mr. Aaron Cohen was at first one of the Treasurers, his colleague being Mr.

Morris Harris, but on his resignation Mr. David L. Jacobs was elected in his stead, and he brought to the work a zeal and a genius for "begging" that helped very considerably to bring the undertaking to a successful issue. Another energetic member of the Building Committee was Mr. Moss Benjamin, then a Warden of the Synagogue. He remained a seatholder of the Synagogue until his death in 1914, and probably created a record in Synagogue honours, holding a seat on the Board of Management of the Old and New Synagogues for over 60 years.

Through the good services of Mr. Abraham Harris, a local resident and a member of the Camberwell Vestry, the Fishmongers' Company had granted a long lease of a plot of land in Albion Place, the name by which the present Heygate Street was then known, and an additional piece of land adjoining was now procured from them.

There was certainly crying need for a new place of worship. The old building was incommodious, dilapidated and unsightly, and was not even a protection against inclement weather, for the roof admitted the rain and the raising of umbrellas during divine worship was no unusual occurrence. It was described as being in ruins, ill-shapen and inconvenient and by no means creditable to the Jewish community. Inconvenient and discreditable it certainly was, for there were hen-runs in the stables situated in the same court as the Synagogue, and mischievous boys, instead of paying due attention to their devotions, had the playful habit of chasing the chickens into the Synagogue, perhaps at the most solemn moments of the services. No wonder, then, that the Jewish press, in its report of the opening of the new Synagogue, said: "It is undeniable that for half a century there has been in Southwark a place of worship whch for dinginess and insalubrity we do not believe had an equal." It accommodated about 110 gentlemen and 36 ladies. There was at the time a gradual influx of Jews from the City, where large numbers of dwelling houses were being demolished to make room for warehouses, and many applications to rent seats had to be refused, nor was there sufficient accommodation for the High Festivals.

An appeal to the Jewish public for assistance, advertised in the *Jewish Chronicle*, was followed by a public meeting on February 25, 1866. The meeting, over which Mr. Meyers presided, was held in the old Synagogue under great difficulties, for the rain freely penetrated the roof, and it was deemed advisable to shorten the proceedings as far

\ as was possible. Resolutions were passed for building a new place of worship " for the large and increasing Jewish population of the South side of London," emphasising the necessity that, in view of the want of Jewish educational institutions in the district, "schools for Jewish children should form a prominent feature in the contemplated new buildings." It should be noted that the only provision for the education of the Jewish youth in the Borough was a private school for boys kept by Mr. Henry Harris, Reader of the Law in the Synagogue, and another for girls kept by Miss Pariente. The latter was maintained by the Baroness de Rothschild, who also subventioned a Sabbath class But the efficiency of the instruction was not regarded as being of a high character, and many children walked every day to and from the Jews' Free School, in Bell Lane, or the School in Greek Street, Soho.

On May 22 the amount collected was only £2,000, whilst the estimates for the Synagogue, Minister's house, and schools, was £5,121. Messrs. N. M. de Rothschild and Sons had, as a result of a visit paid to New Court by Mr. Meyers and the Rev. A. L. Green, Minister of the Central Synagogue, given a donation of £250.

The promoters were disappointed in their hopes that their appeal would meet with a ready and generous response. The three City Synagogues were by no means favourably disposed to the erection of a new Synagogue within two miles of themselves, and offered no encouragement to the project. Many of the residents in the Borough were, for the purpose of burial rights, members of these Synagogues, and such as were not were charged exorbitant rates when sad necessity compelled them to solicit the use of the cemeteries belonging to these Synagogues. Only four years previously the Bayswater Synagogue had been erected, and towards the cost the Great and the New Synagogues had each contributed £1,500. Twelve years earlier the Central Synagogue had been opened, the Great having voted £6,000, and it was just at this time that the latter Synagogue was considering the question of contributing a further similar sum for the removal of this Branch Synagogue to a larger site. About this time, too, a movement was on foot for erecting a Synagogue in North London. It may be that the City Synagogues were influenced in their attitude by the fact that since the end of 1866 they were holding conferences to consider the possibility of a Union of Synagogues, and they may have thought it inopportune and undesirable that they should in any way countenance the establishment of Synagogues other than as branches of their own, and consequently liable to be included in the Union' if this were effected. Anyhow, they declined to mete out to their poorer co-religionists in the South of London the same generous treatment accorded to the rich Jews in the West of the Metropolis. The Great Synagogue contented itself with the reply : " We wish you much joy in your undertaking, but have no funds to g ve you for this purpose.'' The New Synagogue rejected a proposal to vote £100, as well as an amendment to contribute £50. But then so many members of the Borough Synagogue were members of the New.

The Borough people were somewhat sore at the treatment they were receiving ; they felt that they merited something better. They had not kept themselves aloof from the main stream of Jewish life in the Metropolis ; they had, for example, in 1863 contributed the sum of £60 towards the communal collection on behalf of the Lancashire Operatives' Fund, and about £40 for the sufferers by the fire in Monastir, in addition to individual contributions given before the Jewish collections were organised. They were, most of them, seat-holders in one of the City Synagogues, and it was a great hardship that they must subscribe to two Synagogues in order that they might be able to worship conveniently near their homes. They had frequently to complain of the lack of courtesy shown them by the Jewish authorities in the City, events of interest, such as the time of the funeral of communal celebrities, in which they would care to participate, never being officially intimated to them as a congregation. In fact, the only Synagogue recognised by the City Synagogues was that of the " Poor Polish Jews " in Cutler Street, Houndsditch.

In view of the lack of support with which the appeal was meeting, it was determined to abandon for the present the erection of a Minister's house. No public ceremony of laying the foundation stone took place, as this would have " entailed an outlay of upwards of £100, without the probability of any commensurate return in the shape of donations on that occasion,'' and, moreover, the Chief Rabbi had advised that no such ceremony was required. On July 12 the builders, Messrs. Hill and Keddel, were instructed to proceed forthwith with the work. On December 30, a second appeal was resolved upon, the arrangements for this being left in the hands of Mr. D. L. Jacobs. On February 3. 1867, the Rules and Regulations, as drafted by a Sub-committee under the presidency of Mr. M. Davis, were adopted with some modifications, it being resolved that the name of the Synagogue should be the Borough

New Synagogue, propositions to call it the Borough Synagogue, as before, and the South London Synagogue, being rejected.

In spite of the financial difficulty, the consecration of the new building took place on Sunday, April 7, 1867 (Nisan 2, 5627). The clergy of almost every London Synagogue, including the Reform, in Margaret Street, were present. In the procession customary on such occasions, were the Chief Rabbi (Dr. N. M. Adler), the Rev. Dr. Artom (Haham of the Spanish and Portuguese Congregation), Messrs. B. Meyers, S. L. de Symons, H. L. Keeling, S. Moses, D. Benjamin, D. Cohen, and the Wardens (Messrs. Moss Benjamin and M. Harris). The music was composed and conducted by Mr. J. L. Mombach, the famous choirmaster of the Great Synagogue. The afternoon service was read by the Rev. S. Levy, and the dedicatory portions by the Rev. M. B. Levy, Minister of the Western Synagogue, Haymarket, which had lent six Sepharim for use in the circuits around the Synagogue. The Chief Rabbi preached a sermon on the text : Exodus xxxix. 43. Donations to the amount of £306 were announced by the Hon. Secretary, Mr. H. P. Cohen.

In the evening about 60 gentlemen, for the most part belonging to the congregation, met at Radley's Hotel, Bridge Street, and partook of a collation provided at their own expense. It may be mentioned that on March 8, 1868, presentations were made to the honorary officers of the old Synagogue in recognition of the valuable services rendered by them to the congregation while in office. These were Mr. Moss Benjamin and Mr. J. Morris Harris, who had discharged the duties of Wardens for five consecutive years, and Mr. Aaron Cohen, who for upwards of fifty years had served as Treasurer. On March 17, 1872, the congregation further honoured Mr. Cohen by conferring upon him the dignity of ראש הקהל ("Head of the Congregation.")

The following are the names of the Officers, as given in the booklet containing the Order of Service at the Consecration of the Synagogue, and on a tablet placed in the vestibule :—

Wardens: Mr. Moss Benjamin and Mr. Jacob M. Harris.

Treasurer: Mr. Aaron Cohen.

Chairman of Committees: Mr. Barnett Meyers.

Honorary Solicitor: Mr. Saul Solomon.

Trustees: Messrs. Jacob M. Harris, Moss Jacobs, and Moss Harris.

Building Committee: Messrs. Mark Davis, *Chairman;* Morris Harris and David L. Jacobs, *Treasurers;* Henry P. Cohen, *Hon. Secretary;* Moss Benjamin, Jacob M. Harris, and Aaron Cohen.

Secretary to the Synagogue: Mr. P. Ornstien.

When the Synagogue was consecrated, the schools were not completed, nor was the Minister's house begun. On April 22 directions were given for proceeding with these portions of the original scheme. The financial difficulty was obviated by the generosity of Mr. J. J. Ellis, of Brompton, who loaned the Synagogue a sum of £1,000 free of interest for one year.

The Borough Jews were the first among the Ashkenazim to have a Synagogue and school attached to each other, and the close association between the two institutions, perhaps because they are adjacent, has lasted to this day. But it was felt impossible to maintain the school out of the income of the Synagogue. The whole of this would be required for its upkeep, and it was believed—and this belief was afterwards substantiated—that the community would be willing to contribute for educational purposes what it refused for Synagogue building. It was therefore decided that the school should be a separate and distinct institution from the Synagogue, and it was handed over to a Committee on the following terms: They were to pay to the Synagogue by instalments a premium of £1,000, and an initial rent of £60 per annum, this to be decreased from time to time in proportion to the amount of premium already paid, and to be only £10 annually after full payment of the premium. It may prove of interest to those who now administer our Jewish Day Schools and who experience great difficulty in procuring the funds necessary for their maintenance to know that the Borough School was able to repay the whole of the £1,000 by May, 1872, out of surplus income.

The schools, which comprised two stories each of two class-rooms, and which provided accommodation for 150 children, were opened on November 3, 1867, when upwards of 80 boys and girls were enrolled. The parents were expected to pay fees as assessed by the Committee according to their means, but admission was not refused to children whose parents were unable to pay. Mr. B. Berliner, afterwards Minister of the St. John's Wood Synagogue, was elected Headmaster, and Mr. Henry Harris, who had kept the school in Bath Street and was now Reader of the Law at the Synagogue, became his assistant. Miss

Rebecca Samuel was selected as Headmistress and Miss Zox as Assistant. Miss Samuel retained her position down to 1900, when she retired upon an annual pension of £50, still paid by the school, and supplemented by friends of the school.

Before the completion of the Synagogue, consideration had been given to the selection of a Minister. It was generally felt that the officials of the old Synagogue were not competent to perform the duties which other Synagogues were requiring from their Ministers, more particularly in the matter of pulpit instruction which was now forming a regular part of the Sabbath and Festival Services in the London places of worship. Jews' College, together with its school, had been opened in 1855; the first generation of pupils in the School had already passed into the College, and there were a few capable students just completing their course. In a letter dated March 13, 1867, Mr. Barnett Meyers had made suggestions for the future welfare of the congregation, recommending, among other things, that " it should engage a Minister, not a mere singing one, but a learned man who understands what he says and will be able to conduct the school also.'' Applications had been received from Simeon Singer and two others, but the latter withdrew, and Mr. Singer was elected Minister and Secretary on September 1, 1867, entering upon his duties on the New Year Festival. Mr. Singer was barely twenty-one years of age at this time, and there were some who were doubtful of the success of the experiment of appointing so young a man. But he quickly gained the affections of his congregants, and until this day his name is a household word in South London. " To be lovable, live a life of love '' was a saying of his in after years, and it was the principle that guided him, too, during his early years as Minister at the Borough. Much of what follows is taken from the Memoir written by his son-in-law, Dr. Israel Abrahams. His salary was not an adequate provision, and he was forced to teach all day and every day at Jews' College, of which he was for a while Headmaster. His marriage with Charlotte Pyke on April 21, 1868, was the first marriage celebrated in the new Borough Synagogue. This union was one of public interest, as well as personal love, for the wife was associated with all her husband's work and aspirations. Not only did she perform the Secretarial duties for him, but her competent co-operation made it possible for him to serve the community in a host of capacities. Husband and wife were the friends and counsellors of all. As a preacher he enjoyed a great reputation, but Mr. Singer aimed at making others preachers by affording them the opportunity of occupying a pulpit. He originated at the Borough the system of regularly inviting other Ministers or students at Jews' College to preach, and it was at the Borough Synagogue that many a preacher now well known found his first opportunity to reveal his powers, for there was an almost unbroken succession of visiting preachers during the whole period of Mr. Singer's stay in the Borough. When in 1879 he left the Borough Synagogue to become Minister of the New West End Synagogue, then just erected, he and his wife took with them the hearts of many. They knew personally every child in the school, and his interest in the affairs of his first congregation and in its school, in the personal fortunes of its people, only ended with his life. And the affection that he felt for his old congregation was evidenced by his bequeathing to it a legacy more than a quarter of a century after he had left it.

On September 15, the first election of Officers in the new Synagogue took place, the choice falling upon Mr. D. L. Jacobs and Mr. H. P. Cohen as Wardens, and Mr. Saul Solomon as Treasurer. All these had taken a prominent part in the work of erecting the Synagogue, and it was a well-deserved compliment to them and, in particular, to Mr. Jacobs that they should be the first elected officers of the new Synagogue. It may here be stated that although Mr. Jacobs's association with the Synagogue ceased on his removal from the district he never lost his interest in the school, and until his last day was one of its most ardent supporters, and his genial presence was ever welcomed alike by teachers and pupils. An oil painting of his portrait and another of his life-long friend, Mr. Singer, were presented to the Synagogue after their deaths by his brother, Mr. Lewis Jacobs, and hang in the Committee room.

In order to provide a Curtain for the Ark and various Synagogue appurtenances, a Ladies' Committee was constituted, and Mrs. D. L. Jacobs and Mrs. Saul Solomon on its behalf presented the sum of £115 to be expended for this purpose. Mrs. Singer afterwards presented a handsome Chuppah (marriage canopy) as the gift of the ladies of the congregation. This, her own handiwork, is still in use.

In March, 1868, the Synagogue was opened regularly for daily service, and all idea of making it an independent congregation was abandoned, in view of the contemplated Synagogual amalgamation. The monetary difficulties had by no means been overcome, and the congregation was compelled to borrow £2,000 from the bank on the security of the block of buildings comprising the Synagogue, school, and Minister's house, in order to liquidate the building account.

Early in 1869, seats in the Synagogue were allotted for the special use of the schoolchildren, some alterations being made for this purpose.

Very shortly before the High Festivals in that year apprehensions were felt regarding the safety of the Synagogue. Mrs. Singer had observed an ominous caving-in of one of the walls, and had found on the floor of the gallery pieces of plaster which had fallen from the roof. One Sabbath, while the congregation was engaged in silent prayer, a tremendous piece of ceiling fell with a loud crash. There was some alarm for a moment, but no panic; and the service was completed in the customary manner. Immediate steps were taken to ascertain the cause, and although service was held in the Synagogue on the New Year (September 6), it was deemed advisable to engage a hall for worship on the Day of Atonement and during the Festival of Tabernacles, in case an adverse opinion be received in the meanwhile, Mr. M. S. Joseph generously holding himself responsible for the expenses that would thereby be entailed. The government surveyor and the police authorities, however, sanctioned the use of the building, provided that certain works were carried out to add temporarily to its stability. This was done, and the congregation was permitted to assemble in its Synagogue on the Festivals.

The opinion of eminent architects who were consulted was that the defects arose from the roof having been improperly constructed, and supported upon walls of an insufficient thickness to resist the thrust of such a roof. The means they recommended for remedying these defects and ensuring the permanent safety of the erection were the removal of the roof and substitution of a lighter one, and the complete rebuilding of the North and South walls. The architect of the Synagogue, however, preferred the plans he had himself prepared with the aid of surveyors whom he had consulted. He promised that the Synagogue services would not be interrupted, and the Committee agreed that he should carry out the work in his own way, connecting the two defective walls by iron tie-rods of an ornamental character, and strengthening them outside by building buttresses on to them. Much time had been lost during these negotiations, and it was not till Passover that the alterations were completed. It had been found impossible to hold services in the Synagogue itself during the progress of the work, and they were held in the Committee room, and in forwarding him on July 3, 1870, the contribution of £100 which the congregation had promised towards the cost, the Committee intimated to him that in consequence of his delaying the performance of the works connected with the repairs for seven weeks a considerable loss had been incurred by the congregation, and he was asked whether he did not feel himself morally bound to compensate the Synagogue for this. History recordeth not the architect's reply ; certainly the Synagogue accounts contain no entry of any payment by him. Whether the ivy in the Minister's garden destroyed by his workmen was replaced by him as demanded history also telleth not.*

But the troubles in connection with the building were by no means ended. On November 24 an explosion occurred at a house adjacent to the school, the site of which now forms part of the enlarged school, and which was then occupied by Messrs. Pain, the firework manufacturers. The explosion was more alarming than dangerous, although, of course, it caused great excitement at the time, especially amongst the children in their classrooms. Certain damage was done to the Synagogue and school, which was covered by insurance, and again the Synagogue was closed whilst the repairs were being effected.

Nor was this all. There had been continual complaints regarding the lack of a drainage system in the Minister's house, and there had been much sickness amongst its inmates in consequence of this. Mr. Singer was therefore allowed to reside away from Synagogue House, and received an annual sum in commutation of rent. A tenant was found for the house vacated by Mr. Singer, but there was never any improvement in the condition of the drainage : the house remained damp, the garden was a swamp, and all attempts to remedy the defects failed, until finally the house was demolished and a new one erected on a slightly larger site, a portion of a neighbouring garden being purchased for this purpose.

On April 19, 1868, the scheme for the establishment of the United Synagogue was adopted by the members of the several Synagogues originally constituting it, and on July 14, 1870, the " Act for Confirming a Scheme of the Charity Commissioners for the Jewish United Synagogue (33 & 34 Vict., Ch. cxvi.) received the Royal Assent and became part of the law of the land. On November 27, in the same year, the Borough Synagogue opened up communication with the new body, and, at a general meeting on December 12, Mr. M. S. Joseph

---

* It is only fair to state that no architect now living was responsible for the erection of the Synagogue.

urged in forcible terms the importance of union amongst the various congregations. He showed how the difficulties under which their members were labouring as regards burial rights would be removed by amalgamation, since they had no funds for the purchase of a burial ground. The United Synagogue, too, would derive some considerable advantage, for if it took over the Synagogue debt of £1,250 it would receive a building worth £6,000. Mr. Moss Benjamin pointed out how the Borough Synagogue would gain in dignity and importance by uniting with the rich and influential Synagogues. It was decided to approach the United Synagogue, and Messrs. Noah Davis, David Davis, and Barnett Meyers were requested to watch the interests of the Synagogue at the Council. In the statement submitted to the United Synagogue, the following particulars were given : The number of seat-holders was 135 gentlemen and 80 ladies ; there had been a steady increase of income during each of the past three years ; during 1870 this had been £1,250, of which £650 was derived from congregational sources ; the expenditure was £1,110, of which £460 was repayment of capital and interest to bank ; £1,250 was owing to the bank, but this was about to be reduced by £300, the final instalment to be received from the school trustees. The Council of the United Synagogue expressed its willingness to recommend the admission of the Borough Synagogue as a constituent on the conditions that a tax of 30% should be imposed upon the seat-rentals for the general purposes of the institution and that each member should make the customary contribution to the Burial Society in proportion to the rental of his seat. There was nothing objectionable in these financial arrangements, for they applied to all the constituent Synagogues. The Borough Synagogue accepted them on July 16, 1871, their suggestion that the taxation should be on a 20% basis having been declined by the Council. But a month later an extraordinary development occurred : it was discovered that the United Synagogue had no intention of taking over the liability of £950 due to the bank, as the Borough representatives stated they had assumed would be done, and the whole matter was abandoned for a time. There was some idea of obtaining a burial ground of their own, but in November, 1872, the receipt of a letter from the United Synagogue asking for a contribution towards the cost of acquiring a cemetery at Willesden afforded the opportunity to treat for the rental of a portion of this cemetery, as well as to reopen negotiations for amalgamation. At a meeting on November 22, 1872, at which Mr. Lionel L. Cohen, a

Vice-President of the United Synagogue was present, a Sub-Committee to negotiate for admission into the United Synagogue was appointed. This consisted of Messrs. M. S. Joseph and Moss Harris, the Wardens; E. Graumann, Treasurer; and M. Benjamin, D. L. Jacobs, J. M. Harris and S. Solomon. The matter was quickly carried through, for on December 15 a meeting of seatholders passed the necessary resolutions desiring to be admitted into the United Synagogue, and on January 26, 1873, a meeting of the privileged members of that body was held under the presidency of Sir Anthony Rothschild, Bart., at which the formal resolutions by which admission was granted were carried. This was communicated by hand to a meeting of the Committee which was being held the same day, and as the terms of admission were those originally offered by the United Synagogue and did not provide for taking over the liability to the bank, it was decided to have a house-to-house visitation in South London for the purpose of soliciting contributions to supplement those already promised. Donations were obtained from other sources, also, Baron Lionel de Rothschild, M.P., giving £100. On May 20 the sum of £300 was paid off, but the debt was not entirely liquidated till 1876, interest to the bank figuring in each of the annual balance sheets in the interim, the payment of this having been accepted by the United Synagogue, or, at least, not being objected to, as part of the Synagogue's expenditure. By the terms of admission no fewer than fifteen gentlemen who were entitled to be life members of the Borough Synagogue became life members of the Council of the United Synagogue. Of these there is none now surviving.

The minute book of the congregation gives only a bare outline of the course of the negotiations, but it is evident that many difficulties other than those already referred to had to be overcome. The Borough Synagogue was the first to seek and gain admission into the United Synagogue, and great care had to be exercised that no precedent was made to which other Synagogues might later point to the detriment, perhaps, of the United Synagogue. In all the negotiations Mr. Singer was most active, and in a letter from Mr. Lionel L. Cohen their success is described as due to Mr. Singer's instrumentality and as being his personal achievement. As a matter of interest it may be stated that the only other Synagogue already in existence on admission into the United Synagogue was the North London.

During 1876 the Synagogue was renovated, and additional seats were introduced at the back, and between the Wardens' pew and the Ark. The reopening service was held on September 10, the Chief Rabbi, Dr. N. M. Adler, preaching the sermon.

Mr. Singer left the Borough early in 1879. In framing the estimates of income and expenditure for that year the Board of Management had to take into consideration a variety of unfavourable circumstances, among them the actual and prospective removal of a number of liberally contributing members. For some considerable time past much dissatisfaction had been expressed with the lack of efficiency shown by the Choir, which consisted of a contingent of schoolboys, and it was deemed advisable to reorganise this. The resignation of the Minister afforded an opportunity to revise the arrangements with the Synagogue officials. The Rev. P. Ornstien added henceforth to his duties as Second Reader those of Secretary; a sum of £115 was apportioned to the Choir and Choirmaster, and £40 was set aside for a preachers' fund, from which to defray the expenses of a regular rota of visiting preachers. The Rev. M. L. Cohen was appointed Choirmaster on March 16, 1879. When Mr. Ornstien died in 1885, having spent 35 years in the service of the old and new Borough Synagogues, it was decided to combine in one person the offices of Reader, Preacher, and Secretary, and in April, 1886, the Rev. Francis L. Cohen, then Minister in Dublin, was elected to serve in these capacities. Some slight hesitation was felt in making this appointment, on the ground that he was a "Cohen," and therefore unable to perform certain religious rites; but the Delegate Chief Rabbi, whose opinion was sought—and who himself was a "Cohen"—recommended that no candidate otherwise eligible should be disqualified for this reason. Mr. Cohen retained his office till May, 1904, when he received a call to become Rabbi of the Great Synagogue in Sydney, Australia. His ministry in the Borough was an eminently successful one, and he achieved, also, important work for the community in general. Being an authority on traditional Hebrew melody, he edited two publications of Synagogue music which have become standard works in use among the Synagogue Choirs in England and the Colonies. He did much to stimulate the interest of the community in the Regular and Volunteer Forces of the Empire, and became the first Jewish Chaplain to H.M. Forces, originating the annual Military Service on the Festival of Chanucah, the first being held in the Borough Synagogue on December 10, 1893.

He was also one of the founders of the Jewish Lads' Brigade, acting as its Brigade Staff Chaplain.

Mr. Cohen's appointment again brought up the old question of the unsuitability of Synagogue House as a Minister's residence, for he resolutely declined to live in it. Protracted negotiations with the United Synagogue followed, the result of which was that the Council advanced the sum of £585 for the rebuilding of the house, the recoupment of capital and payment of interest on outstanding balances being an annual charge on the local accounts. The Building Committee, however, were by no means satisfied that the house could be built for the estimated sum according to the plans approved of by the Board of Management, and the supervision of the work was therefore entrusted to the Board. The house was ready for occupation in the summer of 1891, and cost about £700, included an outlay of £100 for the purchase of a small plot of ground at the rear of the old house, to permit of an enlarged edifice being put up. This was exclusive of the interior fittings. Towards the entire cost the Synagogue contributed £180 raised by a collection amongst the seatholders.

Towards the end of 1887 the Rev. S. Levy, who had served the congregation since 1862, died, and it was decided that the duties of Reader should be performed henceforth by the Minister, with the assistance of the Choirmaster, the Rev. M. L. Cohen, the salaries of both of these officers being slightly augmented, since it was not deemed advisable to burden the finances of the congregation with the stipend of a First Reader.

It may be within the recollection of many that in May, 1891, a Conference of Ministers was convened by the late Chief Rabbi for the purpose of discussing proposals for modifications in the Synagogue services put forward by certain London Synagogues. It may be of interest to mention here some of the proposals laid before the Conference by the Board of the Borough Synagogue with the approval of its members. The perusal of these will probably raise a smile, but it will show, too, how times have changed, for no one acquainted with the present seatholders would, even for one moment, imagine them recommending such drastic alterations involving, as they do, the abrogation of time-honoured practices and the infringement of Jewish law.

" That the quorum (Minyan) for public worship be three males of full age, instead of ten. That on Friday and Festival evenings, services commence at the exact hour of dusk. That the Shofar be always sounded on the first day of New Year, whether Sabbath or week-day. That inasmuch as an overwhelming majority of members no longer recognise in any way the second days of the New Year and the Three Festivals as Yom Tov, the reading of the ordinary week-day service be permitted on these occasions. That because the ancient objection to instrumental music does not attach to modern keyed instruments, and for various other reasons set forth, the use of the Organ be permitted in Synagogue on any occasion." Needless to say, the late Chief Rabbi did not sanction these " modifications " in the Ritual.

In 1890 a scheme of assessed offerings such as was in force in a few constituent Synagogues was authorised at the Borough, and has served the purpose of substituting a fixed, in place of a fluctuating source of income by distributing the support of the communal burden with more proportional equality than formerly.

Henceforth there is but little of importance to record. Indeed, it may be doubted whether any of the constituent Synagogues of the United Synagogue have any history worth the name when once the pangs attending their birth have passed away. Each is but a unit in the communal organisation of the Metropolis, and the doings of any one of them affect but little the history of Anglo-Jewry, however great the local interest and excitement they arouse. Of such events the Borough Synagogue had many. In 1898, when Mr. John A. Cohen removed from South London, he was presented with an address on vellum setting forth the appreciation of the congregation for his untiring efforts on its behalf during the long period he had been one of its honorary officers. Mr. Cohen was Financial Representative from 1875 to 1877, a Warden from 1878 to 1898, a member of the Board of Management from 1873 to 1902, and of the Council of the United Synagogue from 1875 to 1898, and the Synagogue's Representative at the Board of Deputies from 1883 to 1916. Mrs. Cohen continued to visit the schools regularly and to decorate personally the congregational Succah as she had formerly done, and her husband still sends every year a floral token for this purpose in memory of her. Similar presentations were made in 1908 to Mr. D. Barnard and Mr. B. Lyons, and portraits of Messrs. M. Benjamin, J. A. Cohen, B. Lyons, and the Rev. M. L. Cohen were at various times subscribed for by the Board of Management and now hang in the Committee room.

In 1902 the application of the Board that the Rev. M. L. Cohen should receive the status of an accredited official of the United Synagogue was passed by the Council, having been rejected on more than one occasion previously. The Executive Committee had recommended that the request be not complied with, but the Council recorded its opinion that "the request was fair and reasonable and ought to be granted," and referred the question back to the Executive Committee, which then recommended that the application be agreed to. But in 1908, after the lamented death of the Rev. M. L. Cohen, the Council refused to grant this status to his successor, and the plan was perforce reverted to of engaging a Reader who was not expected to devote the whole of his time to the service of the United Synagogue and the Community, because it was recognised that the "grant" made to him for carrying out the duties of Reader is inadequate as a living wage. In consequence of this policy, changes in the office of Reader occur with greater frequency than is desirable, the Rev. M. Einfeld having been elected in 1908, Rev. S. Anekstien in 1909, and the present incumbent, Rev. E. Frank, in 1912. It is but fair to state that the latter has gone beyond the terms of his agreement, and takes his share in the work of the United Synagogue together with its other Readers.

In 1903, the electric light was installed in the Synagogue, the entire cost being defrayed by the seatholders, past and present. This, together with the purchase of various Synagogue appurtenances, amounted to £200.

In 1905, the Rev. M. Rosenbaum was elected Minister in succession to the Rev. F. L. Cohen; a Ladies' Synagogue Guild was formed, and in 1906, Hebrew and Religion Classes, meeting three times weekly, were established. An attempt to organise classes of this nature had been made some eighteen years previously, but had been abandoned. It was now believed that there was a number of children receiving no religious instruction of any kind, and it was for these and not for the pupils of the Borough Jewish Schools that these classes were intended. Two dozen pupils were enrolled, almost all between the ages of twelve and thirteen, and residing at a considerable distance from the Synagogue, but when, some two years later, these no longer attended school, they ceased to attend these classes also. About this time Hebrew Classes were being opened in the Brixton district, and as the children residing in the more immediate vicinity of the Borough Synagogue either attended the Jewish Schools adjoining or were receiving Hebrew and religious instruction from private tutors, it was not deemed advisable that the classes at the Synagogue should continue with so very small a number of pupils as was available, and failure attended a vigorous attempt to re-establish the classes in 1911.

During the High Festivals of 1905, divine service was held at Brixton, and the promoters approached the Borough Synagogue for assistance in establishing a congregation for the residents of Brixton and the adjacent districts. This again raised the question which had been discussed in 1888, and even earlier, of removing the Borough Synagogue to a site more convenient to the majority of its seatholders, of whom about two-thirds then resided in Brixton and Clapham, or even more southwards. But most of the seatholders chiefly affected showed complete indifference to the matter when it was proposed for consideration at a general meeting, and no action could therefore be taken. The Brixton Congregation and Hebrew Classes were established, and received the support of several members of the Borough Synagogue, who keenly appreciated their own difficulties and those of their neighbours who were attached to no Synagogue. It is quite probable that at this time a more sympathetic view of these difficulties and a statesmanlike policy showing more understanding of the possibilities of the new movement might have obviated the necessity of this, and so altered the course of congregational history in South London. In April, 1908, conferences were held between representatives of the two Synagogues, with the view to their amalgamation, the closing of the Borough Synagogue, and the erection of one which, it was agreed, should not be Citywards of the centre of the Brixton-district. The proposals of the conference were agreed to by the Board of the Borough Synagogue, but rejected by that of the Brixton Synagogue, who stated that they did "not regard the time as ripe for amalgamation." At the request of the Brixton Synagogue conferences were again held at the end of 1909, and a joint meeting was also held between representatives of the two congregations and the honorary officers of the United Synagogue. The latter were of opinion that the suggestion to amalgamate the two congregations with the Brixton Synagogue as a branch of the Borough—in other words, the formation of one congregation with two places of worship—was impracticable, and requested the views of the Board of the Borough Synagogue as to the transfer of their Synagogue to the locality of Brixton. But during the interval of four years that had elapsed since 1905, a complete change had taken place. Many seatholders of the Borough Synagogue had joined that at Brixton, others had removed from South London, a considerable number of co-religionists had migrated from East London into the Walworth and Tower Bridge districts, so that now two-thirds of the members resided in the locality contiguous to the Synagogue, whereas four years previously this proportion had resided in the vicinity of Brixton and Clapham. The Board therefore expressed itself against the closing of the Synagogue, and the Brixton congregation proceeded upon the even tenor of its path, going "from strength to strength." When, in 1911, it sought the assistance of the United Synagogue in the erection of a place of worship as an Associate Synagogue of the Union, the Board of the Borough held that for various reasons this was not desirable, but offered no opposition to its erection as a Constituent Synagogue, with the same status and obligations as their own Synagogue. This was agreed to, and the Brixton Synagogue was opened in 1913 as a constituent of the United Synagogue.

In 1914 a Free Funeral Society was established, similar to those existing at some other Synagogues. An attempt to form one in 1901 had proved unsuccessful.

The local poor, of whom there are but few, are cared for by the South London Jewish Local Charity, which was founded in 1896 at the suggestion of Mr. Jacob Woolf. It makes grants of small gifts and loans to the deserving poor, cases requiring more generous treatment than the Society can afford being dealt with by the Jewish Board of Guardians, for which Mr. J. Bernberg, the Headmaster of the School, acts as honorary visitor in South London.

The appeals of the War Charities have not fallen upon deaf ears. Collections have been made for the Red Cross and for local funds, and a Hostel for Jewish Refugees from Belgium was opened where some two dozen persons were maintained for over a year until they became self-supporting. The members of the Synagogue have contributed generously to the Fund for the Relief of the Jewish Victims of the War in Russia, eleven sum of £50 each having been sent to the head committee. A total of more than £1,000 has been collected for these two specifically Jewish purposes, almost all of it by means of small weekly or monthly amounts. These successful efforts have been made possible only through regularity in calling upon the numerous subscribers during a period exceeding two years, and the self-sacrificing work of the honorary collectors, Messrs. B. Cohen, A. Emdon, P. A. Norman, H. Harris, and H. Abraham, Miss Rosenbaum, and Miss Silverston, are deserving of the highest commendation.

Our brief account of the Synagogues in "the Borough" is now completed. In this, its Jubilee year, the Borough New Synagogue has a record membership. The Jewish population is of a floating character, for Walworth and its surroundings is not a residential district, and offers no inducement to well-to-do people to settle within its borders. There is, it is true, a continuous stream of newcomers who believe that South London offers them an excellent field for a business venture, but disillusionment soon comes, and unless they possess sufficient capital to enable them to hold out until they are well established they quickly return whence they came. How great is this migratory movement may be gathered from the fact that during the past eight years no fewer than 244 gentlemen and 127 ladies have become seat-holders in the Synagogue, being more than sufficient to fill every seat, and yet the present membership is only 22 gentlemen and 32 ladies in excess of that at the beginning of this period, being 202 gentlemen and 108 ladies, leaving only 11 seats vacant in each part of the Synagogue.

The Borough Synagogue is not one of the "surplus" Synagogues; indeed, if every seat were occupied at the scheduled rentals it would still be a "deficit" Synagogue. But it serves a distinct and important function in a metropolitan district, where there are otherwise but few Jewish influences and agencies at work. The Southern boroughs are not thickly populated by our co-religionists; they contain no streets where, as in the East and some parts of the North of London, the Jewish residents form the predominating element in number. Jewish solidarity, therefore, and Jewish "public opinion" do not exist to any great extent, and the only Jewish influences under which many families come are those of the Synagogue and the school.

But with the change in the character of the Jewish population new needs have arisen, and it should be the duty of the Synagogue to create new agencies to supply these needs. The larger Jewish Friendly Societies have quickly appreciated the possibilities of the new conditions, and the Order "Shield of David" has a men's Lodge, with a branch for boys, and the Order "Achei B'rith and Shield of Abraham" has Lodges both for men and women, and there are signs that all these may become potent agencies for good apart from the Friendly Society section of their work. The Ministers of the Synagogue keep in close touch with these organisations in order to cement the bond which should exist, and it is hoped that a very close association between them may be effected.

One striking peculiarity of communal organisation should not be passed over without mention, for a similar condition probably does not exist elsewhere in London. The two constituent Synagogues in South London draw the larger portion of their membership from an area covering about eighteen square miles, and the great distances at which the seatholders reside from the Synagogues make their attendances at the services on Sabbaths and Festivals almost impossible, to say nothing of economical reasons which make regular participation in public worship on these days very difficult. Parochial visiting is consequently the more essential if the tie between the Synagogue and its members is to be something more than a nominal one, beginning and ending in a monetary contribution, and if new settlers are to be attracted to the Synagogue. And yet a vicious policy was begun in South London and has been continued there alone, being exemplified only in the staffing of the Borough and the Brixton Synagogues, of appointing to each only one minister, who is expected to devote to Synagogue work the whole of his time, which really means such time as may remain after the performance of secretarial duties and the visitation of public institutions. This is a short-sighted policy, which brings a host of evils in its train, the results of which may still be noted by those who are conversant with local conditions and know how to trace them to their causes.

A fresh migration of our co-religionists into both the business and residential portions of South London is now slowly proceeding, and it is for the community to see to it that the old system with all its attendant evils should not be perpetuated to the detriment of the religious welfare of the present and future generations of Jews in " the Borough."

Officers of the Synagogue

Preachers:

1867–1879 REV. S. SINGER.
1885–1904 REV. F. L. COHEN.
1905— REV. M. ROSENBAUM.

Readers:

1862–1887 REV. S LEVY.	1908–1909 REV. M. EINFELD.
1862–1885 REV. P. ORNSTIEN.	1909–1912 REV. S. ANEKSTIEN.
1888–1907 REV. M. L. COHEN.	1912— REV. E. FRANK.

Officers of the Prospect Place Synagogue

(LIST EXTRACTED FROM THE "LAWS OF THE BOROUGH NEW SYNAGOGUE," 1868.

Wardens:

WOLF SIMMONDS, ESQ. (the late).	HYAM HYAMS, ESQ.
LYON LEVY, ESQ.	HYAM LEVY, ESQ.
JONAS MICHAEL, ESQ. (the late).	SAMUEL MORSE, ESQ.
EMANUEL SOLOMONS, ESQ. (the late).	SOLOMON MYERS, ESQ.
	SIMON JOSEPH, ESQ.
M. MOSS, ESQ. (the late).	HENRY BENJAMIN, ESQ.
MORRIS HARRIS, ESQ.	MOSS BENJAMIN, ESQ.
BENJAMIN PHILLIPS, ESQ.	JACOB M. HARRIS, ESQ.
JOSEPH JOSEPH, ESQ.	

Treasurer:

AARON COHEN, ESQ.

Officers of the Borough New Synagogue, Heygate Street

Wardens :

1867 1869–1870 1875–1878	M. BENJAMIN, ESQ.	1878–1880 1881–1898	J. A. COHEN, ESQ.
1867	J. M. HARRIS, ESQ.	1880–1892	H. J. SOLOMONS, ESQ.
1867–1869	D. L. JACOBS, ESQ.	1892–1900	J. WOOLF, ESQ.
1867–1868	H. P. COHEN, ESQ.	1898–1900	A. MAY, ESQ.
1868–1869	J. L. SIMMONDS, ESQ.	1900–1902	A. J. HERON, ESQ.
1869–1871	MARK DAVIS, ESQ.	1900–1909	B. LYONS, ESQ.
1871–1872	L. BENJAMIN, ESQ.	1902–1903 1905–1912	A. ISAACS, ESQ.
1871–1875	M. S. JOSEPH, ESQ.	1903–1905 1912—	H. BERNHARDT COHEN, ESQ.
1872–1875	MOSS HARRIS, ESQ.	1912–1913	E. TELLER, ESQ.
1875–1881	J. SALAMON, ESQ.	1913—	J. BERNBERG, ESQ.

Treasurers and Financial Representatives :-

1867	A. COHEN, ESQ.	1881–1889	S. WEINGOTT, ESQ.
1867–1869 1879–1881	SAUL SOLOMON, ESQ.	1889–1891	D. DAVIS, ESQ.
		1891–1896	A. LEON, ESQ.
1869–1871	M. S. JOSEPH, ESQ.	1896–1900	B. LYONS, ESQ.
1871–1872	MOSS HARRIS, ESQ.	1900–1907 1909–1911	D. BARNARD, ESQ.
1872–1873	E. GRAUMANN, ESQ.		
1873–1875 1877–1879	*H. B. BARNARD, ESQ.	1907–1909	M. SILVERSTON, ESQ.
		1911–1913	J. BERNBERG, ESQ.
1875–1877	J. A. COHEN, ESQ.	1913—	A. A. LOGETTE, ESQ.

* The First Financial Representative, 1873.

Representatives at the Council of the United Synagogue :

1873–1875	S. JOSEPH, ESQ.	1899–1903 1905–1913	H. B. COHEN, ESQ.
1875–1877 1879–1883	N. BRAUNSTEIN, ESQ.	1903–1905	DR. A. GROSS.
1875–1877	E. HYMAN, ESQ.	1903–1905	A. ISAACS, ESQ.
1877–1879	J. A. COHEN, ESQ.	1905–1907	M. SILVERSTON, ESQ.
1877–1889, 1891–1899	E. A. COHEN, ESQ.	1907–1911	J. BERNBERG, ESQ.
		1911–1913	M. DAVIS, ESQ.
1883–1889	D. DAVIS, ESQ.	1913—	P. BRYMAN, ESQ.
1889–1891	H. LEON, ESQ.	1913—	E. S. ISRAEL, ESQ.
1889–1903	H. M. HARRIS, ESQ.		

9 781169 507852